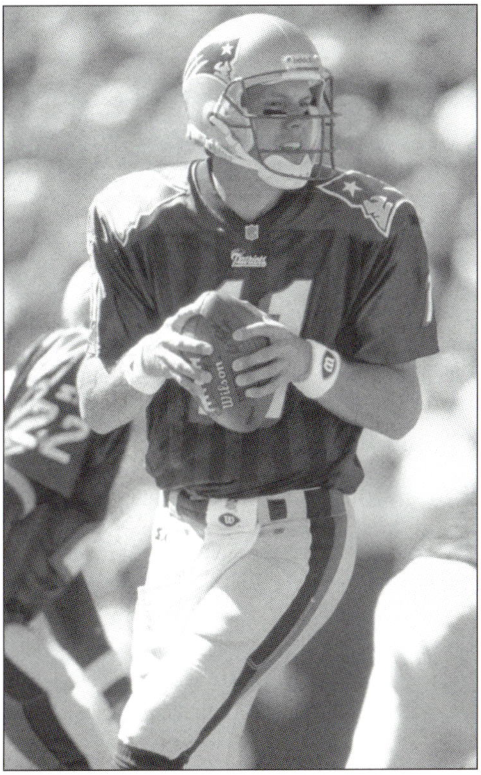
Wilson

GREAT RIVER REGIONAL LIBRARY

CREATIVE EDUCATION · NEW ENGLAND PATRIOTS · JULIE NELSON

Published by Creative Education
123 South Broad Street, Mankato, Minnesota 56001
Creative Education is an imprint of The Creative Company

Designed by Rita Marshall

Photos by: Active Images, Allsport USA, AP/Wide World Photos, SportsChrome

Copyright © 2001 Creative Education.
International copyrights reserved in all countries.
No part of this book may be reproduced in any form without written
permission from the publisher.
Printed in the United States of America.

Library of Congress Cataloging-in-Publication Data

Nelson, Julie.
New England Patriots / by Julie Nelson.
p. cm. — (NFL today)
Summary: Traces the history of the team from its beginnings through 1999.
ISBN 1-58341-050-3

1. New England Patriots (Football team)—History—Juvenile literature. [1. New England Patriots (Football team)—History. 2. Football—History.] I. Title. II. Series: NFL today (Mankato, Minn.)

GV956.N36N45   2000
796.332'64'0974461—dc21   99-015745

First edition

9 8 7 6 5 4 3 2 1

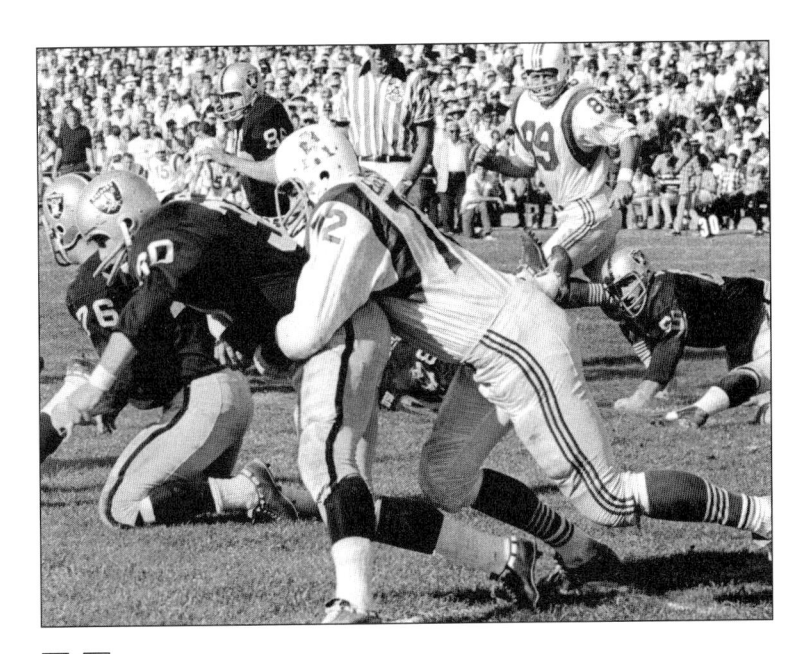

Many of the first American colonists who left England for the New World ended up settling in what is now the northeastern United States. These settlers called the land New England after their former home. Even today, the northeastern United States is commonly referred to as New England, a region that includes Massachusetts, New Hampshire, Connecticut, Rhode Island, Vermont, and Maine.

The largest city in New England is Boston, Massachusetts. Since its founding in the 1600s, Boston has been the center of political and economic life in New England. Boston was also the scene of many famous events leading up to the Rev-

A Patriots great, linebacker Nick Buoniconti.

olutionary War, including the Boston Tea Party and Paul Revere's legendary ride to warn colonists of a British attack.

Those American colonists who wanted independence from British rule were called patriots, and the Boston area was home to many of them. Today, Boston is still home to Patriots, though they are no longer fighting the British. These Patriots are struggling to make it to the top of the standings in the National Football League.

When the New England team was first formed in 1960, it was known as the Boston Patriots. The Patriots joined seven other teams as original members of the American Football League. Boston had some success in the AFL's first years. In 1963, the Patriots tied the Buffalo Bills for first place in their division, then crushed the Bills 26–8 in the playoffs. When Boston met San Diego to play for the AFL title, however, the Chargers trounced the Patriots 51–10. It would be a long 22 years before the Patriots would again reach a league championship game.

Gino Cappelletti kicked 17 field goals and led the Patriots with 768 receiving yards.

NANCE KNOCKS 'EM OVER

The Patriots finished second in their division in 1964 before struggling to a 4–8–2 record in 1965—the worst record in their six-year existence. Luckily, the 1965 season also marked the arrival of a gifted player who could help the ailing Patriots: Syracuse University running back Jim Nance.

When Nance reported to the Patriots' training camp in the summer of 1965, Patriots coaches understood why "Big Bo" was their new fullback's nickname. Nance weighed in at 260 pounds—heavier than most of the Patriots' linemen. Coach

Hard-hitting outside linebacker Chris Slade.

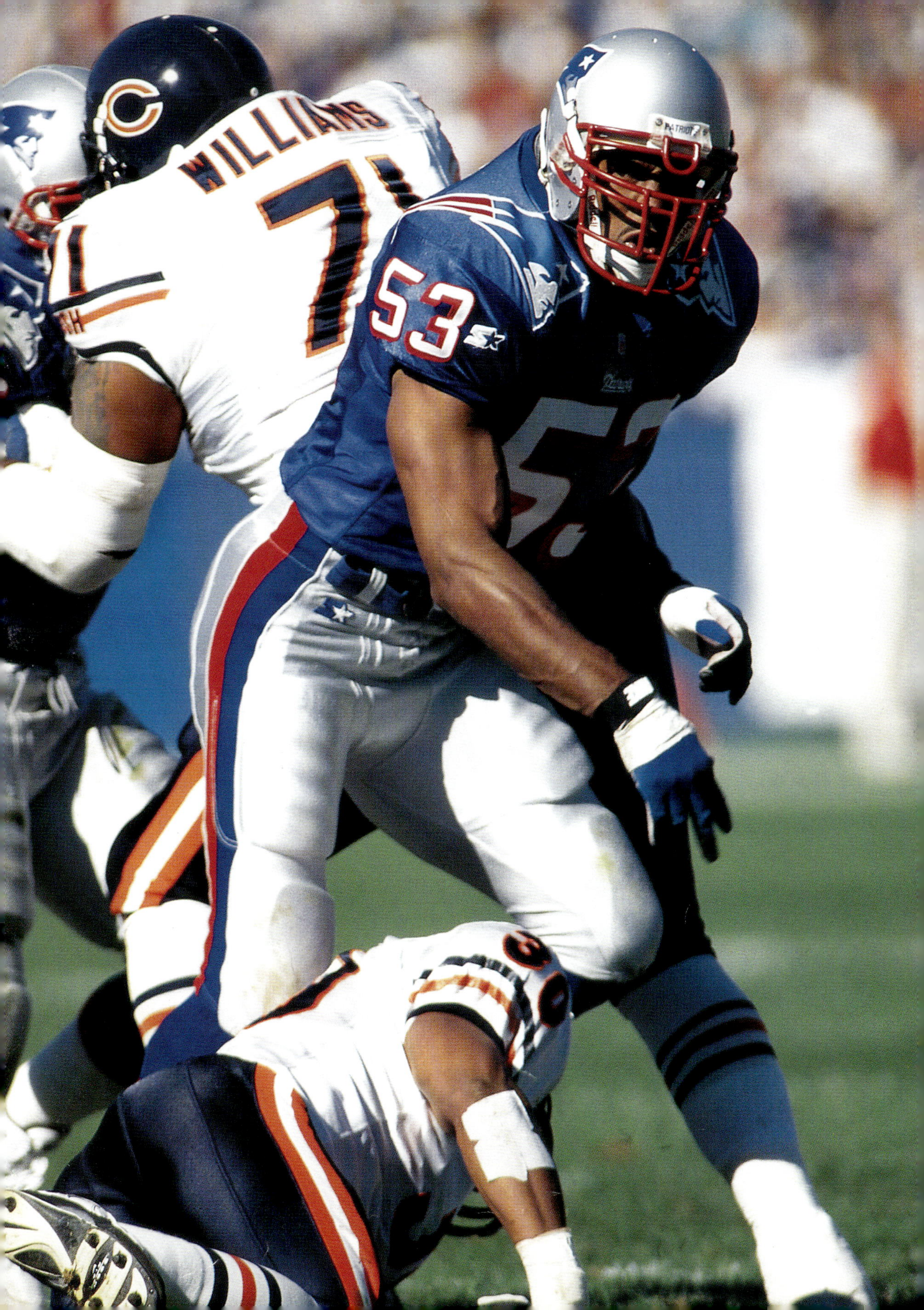
WILLIAMS
71
53

1967

Big fullback Jim Nance powered through defenses for 1,216 yards.

Mike Holovak gave Nance a choice: "You block pretty well. How would you like to be switched to guard? If you don't get your weight down in a hurry, next week you start working out with the linemen."

Nance didn't want to play guard, so he quickly dropped 14 pounds in a week to win the position as starting fullback. A year later, he reported to training camp weighing a trim 235 pounds and eager for a great season. Nance's hard work paid off as he tore through defenses for an AFL-record 1,458 rushing yards. The Patriots were on their way back to the top, and Nance was one of the league's most feared backs.

Nance made a practice of running over, not around, people. "I've been noticing that when a guy hits me head-on, he's not quite so quick to hit me the next time," Nance explained. "So I keep running at him, and pretty soon he wants to turn his shoulder. Then I know I've got him. When a man turns his shoulder on me, I'm going to get past him before he turns back."

Even Nance couldn't save his team from a losing season in 1967, however, when the Patriots turned in a dismal 3–10–1 showing that earned them a last-place finish. Boston also became notorious for its poor fan attendance, which was so low that the team hadn't even invested in building a permanent home field. By the time the AFL and NFL merged into one league in 1970, the Patriots had called five different fields home in their first 10 years.

In 1971, the team finally adopted Schaefer Stadium in Foxboro, Massachusetts, as its home field. In honor of the team's new location on the outskirts of Boston, team owner Billy Sullivan changed its name to the New England Patriots.

HANNAH AND GROGAN TAKE CHARGE

Over the next few years, the Patriots added several players who would make them winners again. The first of these additions was offensive lineman John Hannah, who arrived in 1973. At 6-foot-2 and 265 pounds, Hannah was amazingly strong, but he also had remarkable speed and agility for a man his size. This natural ability, along with great intensity, made Hannah one of the best offensive linemen of all time.

Baltimore Colts lineman Jim Parker, a Pro Football Hall-of-Famer and another of the greatest offensive linemen ever to play in the NFL, praised Hannah as "the only one out there who can do it all—every aspect. . . . I sure would have enjoyed playing alongside him."

Once Hannah became a perennial All-Pro, opponents began looking for ways to beat the big lineman. The Patriots' star, however, relished the challenge. "One thing I found out," Hannah said, "was that the guy you'd see on film wasn't always the same player you'd meet on the field. If they thought you were one of the best, they'd get all fired up and play over their heads."

Hannah successfully fended off almost all attackers, but the team had a hard time finding a quality quarterback to line up behind him. After a 3–11 finish in 1975, the Patriots turned to backup quarterback Steve Grogan, an experienced player who knew the Patriots' system well.

The gamble paid off. With Grogan leading the offense, the Patriots turned their fortunes around and soared to an 11–3 record in 1976. Grogan had both a strong arm and

John Hannah began his climb to the Hall of Fame with his first Pro Bowl berth.

Quarterback Steve Grogan led the Patriots . . .

... *with the help of runner John Stephens.*

1977

Wide receiver Darryl Stingley was the Patriots' top deep threat, racking up 657 yards.

quick feet, and his scrambling ability made him one of the league's most dangerous quarterbacks. "I've always believed in trying to take advantage of the abilities your players have," Patriots coach Chuck Fairbanks said, "and Steve is a threat as a runner."

Grogan was a driving force behind the Patriots. "He's our leader, our motivator," Hannah said. "When we need big plays, he comes up with them. There's only a few quarterbacks who will do what Steve does now. He holds that ball. He'll sit there, hold it, he'll get that lick, and then throw. It makes you want to give up a little bit of your life for him."

Perhaps Grogan's biggest challenge was adjusting to his new-found fame. A native of rural Kansas, Grogan struggled to adjust to life in the big city. "We don't have anything like Boston in Kansas," he once explained. "I'm not used to going out shopping or to the movies and always being recognized. How do I handle it? I handle it by staying home."

The shy Kansan may have tried to dodge his fame, but New England fans were thrilled with their new hero. The Patriots reached the playoffs in 1976 and almost pulled off a huge upset. In their first postseason game, they met the Raiders in Oakland. The Raiders, who had expected to roll over New England, were shocked when the Patriots took a 21–10 lead early in the game's second half. Raiders quarterback Kenny Stabler brought his team back, however, in a fourth-quarter rally that clinched a 24–21 victory and brought an end to one of the most thrilling NFL games in years. The Raiders marched on to win the Super Bowl, but many football experts were convinced that New England was the team of the future in the AFC.

CHANGES, HEARTBREAKS, AND A SUPER BOWL

New England fans had good reason for high expectations. The Patriots had a bright collection of young stars to help Grogan and Hannah. Offensive leaders included fullback Sam Cunningham, wide receiver Darryl Stingley, tackle Leon Gray, and tight end Russ Francis. The equally-loaded Patriots defense was anchored by linemen Julius Adams and Ray Hamilton, while linebackers Steve Nelson and Rod Shoate stuffed opponents along the line. Two other bright prospects, cornerback Mike Haynes and safety Tim Fox, joined the roster in 1976.

The 1977 NFL draft yielded two more stars for the Patriots. University of Texas running back Raymond Clayborn came

1979

Ball-hawking cornerback Raymond Clayborn led the defense with five interceptions.

Hall of Fame cornerback Mike Haynes.

1980

Tight end Russ Francis caught eight passes for touchdowns.

to New England as a cornerback, where he and Mike Haynes became a prized pair of man-to-man pass defenders. Stanley Morgan, a sprinter from the University of Tennessee, joined Darryl Stingley to form a speedy wide receiver duo.

Unfortunately, hopes of a 1977 Super Bowl season ended with preseason contract disputes between Hannah and Gray and team management. Hannah eventually agreed to a richer contract and played, but Gray was traded to New Orleans. The team faltered, losing four games early in the 1977 season. Although the Patriots recovered and ended the season a respectable 9–5, they failed to make the playoffs.

Despite the disappointing 1977 season, many sportswriters were convinced the Patriots would make it back to the playoffs in 1978. Sadly, tragedy struck in a preseason game against the Oakland Raiders. Steve Grogan lobbed a pass to Darryl Stingley. As Stingley jumped high for the catch, he was drilled in midair by Oakland safety Jack Tatum. Stingley hit the turf hard and didn't get up. Doctors found that Stingley's neck was broken, abruptly ending his career and paralyzing him from the neck down.

Stingley's accident motivated the Patriots to play their best in the hopes of lifting the spirits of their fallen teammate. This momentum brought them the AFC Eastern Division title in 1978, but the Patriots lost their first playoff game to the Houston Oilers, 31–14. Coach Chuck Fairbanks resigned, leaving a winning team for his successor, Ron Erhardt.

After three frustrating seasons, New England owner Billy Sullivan fired Erhardt and brought in Ron Meyer, who soon traded veterans Russ Francis, Rod Shoate, and Tim Fox in exchange for future draft choices. With the draft choices,

14

A perennial Pro-Bowler, linebacker Andre Tippett.

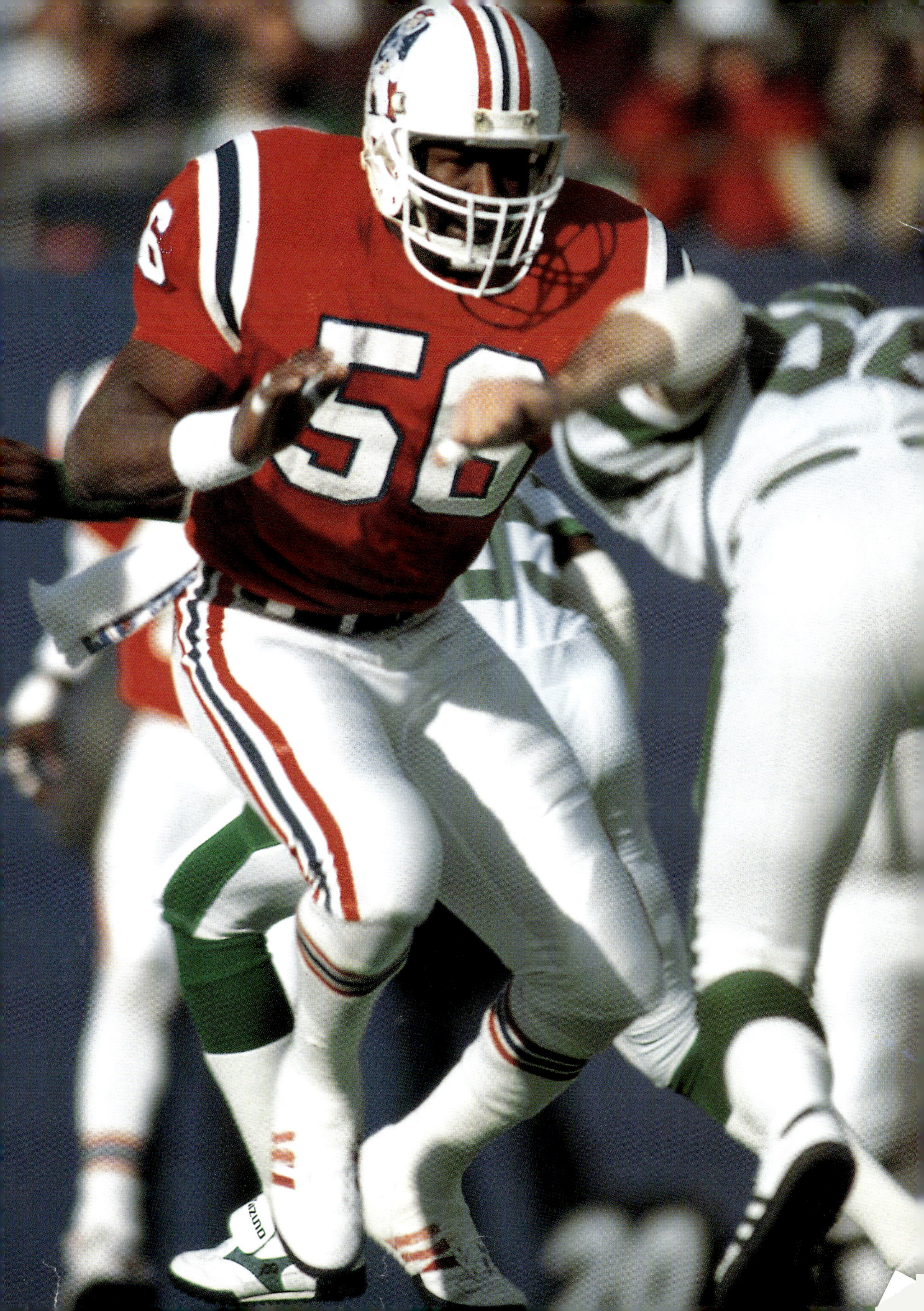
56

Bruising fullback Sam Cunningham.

Meyer then brought star defenders Kenneth Sims and Andre Tippett to New England. In 1983, Meyer used another draft choice to add quarterback Tony Eason to the team. Meyer's changes did not produce an immediate winner, however, and he was fired in 1984.

New coach Raymond Berry brought many years of football experience—both as a player and a coach—to New England. In 1985, Berry's experience paid off. Steve Grogan, who battled Tony Eason to retain his quarterback job and endured the boos of angry Patriots fans, came back from a string of down years to record a stellar season in 1985. "I don't care for being booed," Grogan said. "I want to prove myself to the people here."

Grogan led the Patriots to a comeback win over Cincinnati in the regular season's final week to clinch a playoff spot. Coach Berry, eager to emphasize a running game in the playoffs, brought in Eason to quarterback the team. Eason mainly handed off to running backs Craig James and Tony Collins, who moved the ball well enough to lead New England over the New York Jets, Los Angeles Raiders, and Miami Dolphins in the playoffs. After a decade of trials and tribulations, the Patriots had finally reached the Super Bowl.

The Patriots got off to a promising start against the Chicago Bears in Super Bowl XX, kicking a field goal barely a minute into the game (the fastest score in Super Bowl history). Unfortunately, the powerful Bears then took over, scoring the next 44 points. Grogan, who replaced a struggling Eason in the second quarter, passed for only one Patriots touchdown against the stingy Bears defense as Chicago won in a 46–10 rout.

Head coach Raymond Berry led New England to an 11–5 record.

Halfback Curtis Martin shared Grogan's determination (pages 18-19).

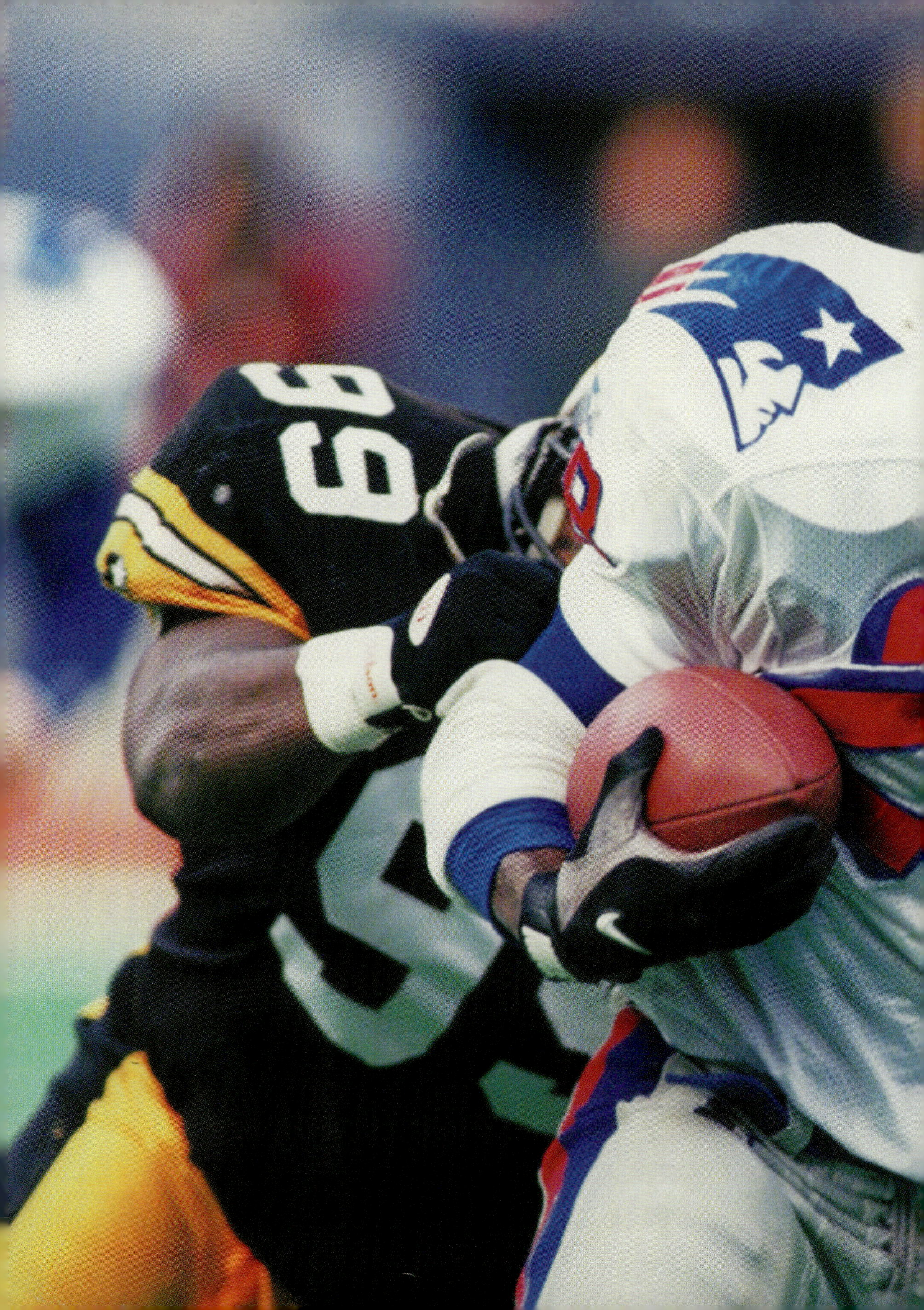
99

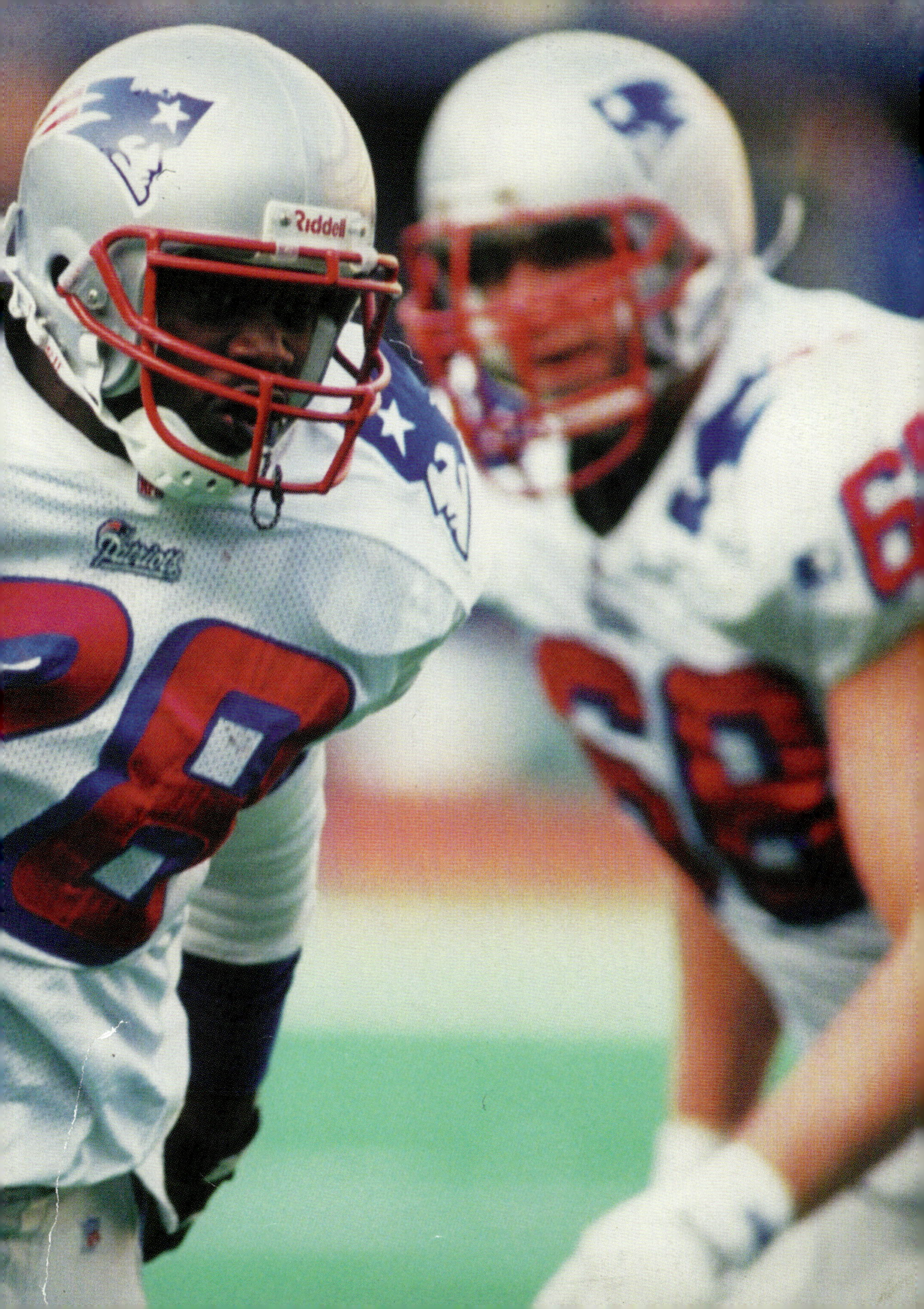
Riddell

STANLEY AND STEPHENS BECOME STARS

Veteran receiver Stanley "Steamer" Morgan led New England in receiving yards (502).

As the Patriots approached the 1986 season, their prospects looked bright when Stanley "Steamer" Morgan arrived at training camp in great shape. Morgan had made two trips to the Pro Bowl in the early 1980s, but coach Ron Meyer had rarely given Morgan much playing time. Morgan, angered by the change, developed a bad attitude. "I got lazy," he said, "and got into some bad habits."

But Morgan wasn't finished yet. When Coach Berry took over, he saw that Morgan still had great potential. Morgan regained his confidence and his health, turning in an amazing 1986 season. "I was excited about playing football again," Morgan declared, and his excitement showed. He set a team record with 84 pass receptions, 10 of them for touchdowns. In nine games, he caught passes for at least 100 yards.

Morgan's last great clutch grab in the 1986 season reminded skeptics why the 10-year veteran was so valuable to the Patriots. With 44 seconds left to play, New England and Miami were tied 27–27, and New England had the ball on the Miami 30-yard line. On the next play, Grogan faded back and lobbed a long pass up the right sideline into Morgan's waiting hands—in the end zone. The touchdown won the game for the Patriots and clinched a playoff berth. Unfortunately, they went on to fall to the Denver Broncos, 22–17.

Over the next two seasons, the Patriots' fortunes declined. By 1989, however, there was again reason for optimism in New England. The New England defense contained plenty of talent, including Andre Tippett—who honed his skills by practicing the martial arts—and cornerback Ronnie Lippett.

On the offensive side, running back John Stephens, a rookie in 1988, had proven to be a pleasant surprise. Although he had drawn little attention in college, he ran for 1,168 yards in 1988 to finish second in the AFC in rushing and earn a Pro Bowl berth.

Unfortunately, the bad luck that had dogged the Patriots returned in 1989. Tippett was hurt in a preseason game and missed the entire season. The Patriots' defense was often torn apart during his absence. At age 36, Grogan was often banged up and in need of a backup, but the Patriots had no other effective quarterback. Stephens also played most of the season with injuries. By the end of the season, New England's record was a disappointing 5–11, marking the Patriots' first losing season in eight years.

Linebacker Johnny Rembert anchored the Patriots defense and earned a spot in the Pro Bowl.

Powerful offensive lineman Bruce Armstrong.

A superb receiver, tight end Ben Coates.

Aiming High in the 1990s

Rod Rust, who had been the defensive coordinator for New England's Super Bowl team, was brought in to replace Raymond Berry as head coach after the 1989 season. Fortunately, most of the Patriots had healed up by that time as well. In 1990, Tippett returned to the regular lineup; John Stephens was back at full strength; and a determined Steve Grogan beat out the young quarterbacks who were brought in to replace him.

As it turned out, though, 1990 would be one of the Patriots' worst seasons ever. Finishing with a 1–15 record, the Patriots had gone from embarrassing to horrible. Rust was dismissed and a new head coach, Dick MacPherson, came on board in 1991. The change led to little improvement, however. New England finished 1991 with a 6–10 record and dropped to 2–14 in 1992.

Bill Parcells—who had led the New York Giants to two Super Bowl victories—took over as head coach in 1993. At that point, the Patriots had suffered through four losing seasons in a row. Parcells came to New England determined to reverse that tailspin and mold another winning team. He began by using the Patriots' number one pick in the 1993 NFL draft to snare star quarterback Drew Bledsoe out of Washington State. The 21-year-old Bledsoe soon began to show the determination and coolness under pressure that would make him a star in the AFC.

Bledsoe and Parcells developed a unique relationship built on their mutual respect for each other's abilities. Still,

1 9 9 3

Tackle Bruce Armstrong led an offensive line that gave up only 23 sacks all season.

Special teams star David Meggett racked up 1,347 yards returning kicks and punts.

the demanding coach knew that his young quarterback had a lot of untapped potential. "He's learned some things," Parcells admitted, "but not all of the things he does are good." Bledsoe, known for his relaxed, easygoing nature, praised his coach but said that Parcells "turns the pressure up in practice when we're not winning. That's the hard part. You almost never see me fired up and ticked off. I still look at this as fun."

Fans had fun as well watching Bledsoe develop. In 1994, his second NFL season, Bledsoe attempted a record 691 passes and completed 400, only four short of Warren Moon's all-time NFL completion record. He passed for an amazing 4,555 yards that season—one of the highest totals in league history—and became the youngest quarterback ever elected

One of the AFC's top defensive ends, Willie McGinest.

to the Pro Bowl. Behind Bledsoe's breakthrough season, the Patriots finished 10–6 and returned to the playoffs at last.

New England dipped to a 6–10 record the next season. Still, with Bledsoe and other young standouts such as rookie running back Curtis Martin, the Patriots seemed to be heading in the right direction.

The Patriots began the 1996 season with a bit of controversy. New England was scheduled to pick seventh in the NFL draft, and Parcells felt that the team needed to add a talented defensive player. Team owner Robert Kraft disagreed, however, and used the pick to select Terry Glenn, a standout receiver from Ohio State. Although the decision was at first a source of frustration for Parcells, it would prove to be an excellent move.

On the field, Glenn flourished in New England's potent offense, racking up 1,132 receiving yards and setting a new NFL rookie record for receptions (90). Bledsoe once again put up impressive numbers—4,086 passing yards and 27 touchdowns—and Curtis recorded his second straight 1,000-yard rushing season to round out the attack.

Behind these efforts, the Patriots went 11–5 during the regular season, earning their first AFC East title since 1986. From there, they coasted through the playoffs, crushing Pittsburgh 28–3 for the first home playoff win in franchise history, then beating Jacksonville 20–6. New England was finally back in the Super Bowl.

New England's opponent in Super Bowl XXXI was the Green Bay Packers, led by quarterback Brett Favre, the league's Most Valuable Player for a second straight year. The first quarter was a showcase of offensive power as the teams

1996

Coach Bill Parcells brought the Patriots back to prominence with an AFC championship.

Game-breaking wide receiver Terry Glenn (pages 26-27).

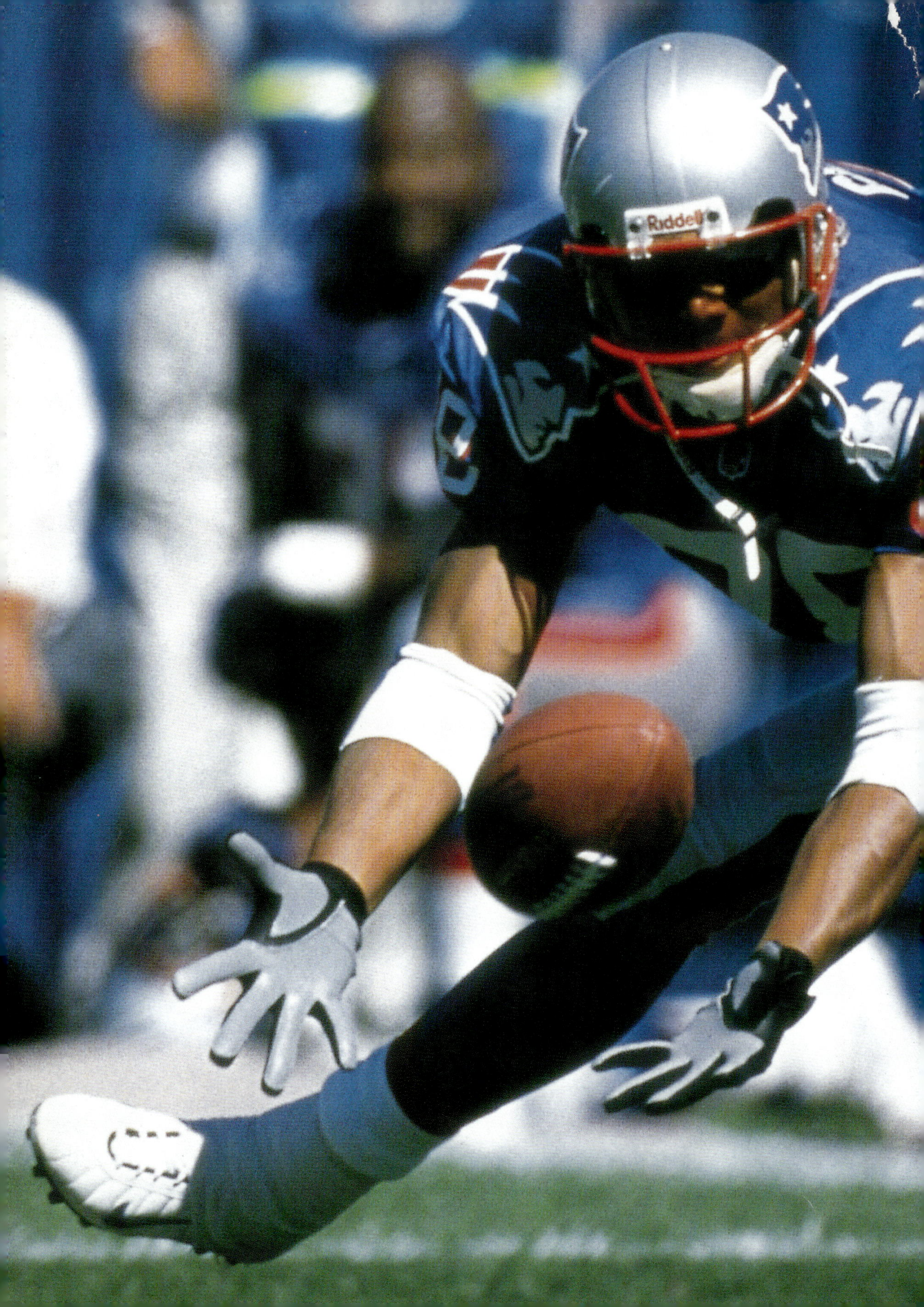
Riddell

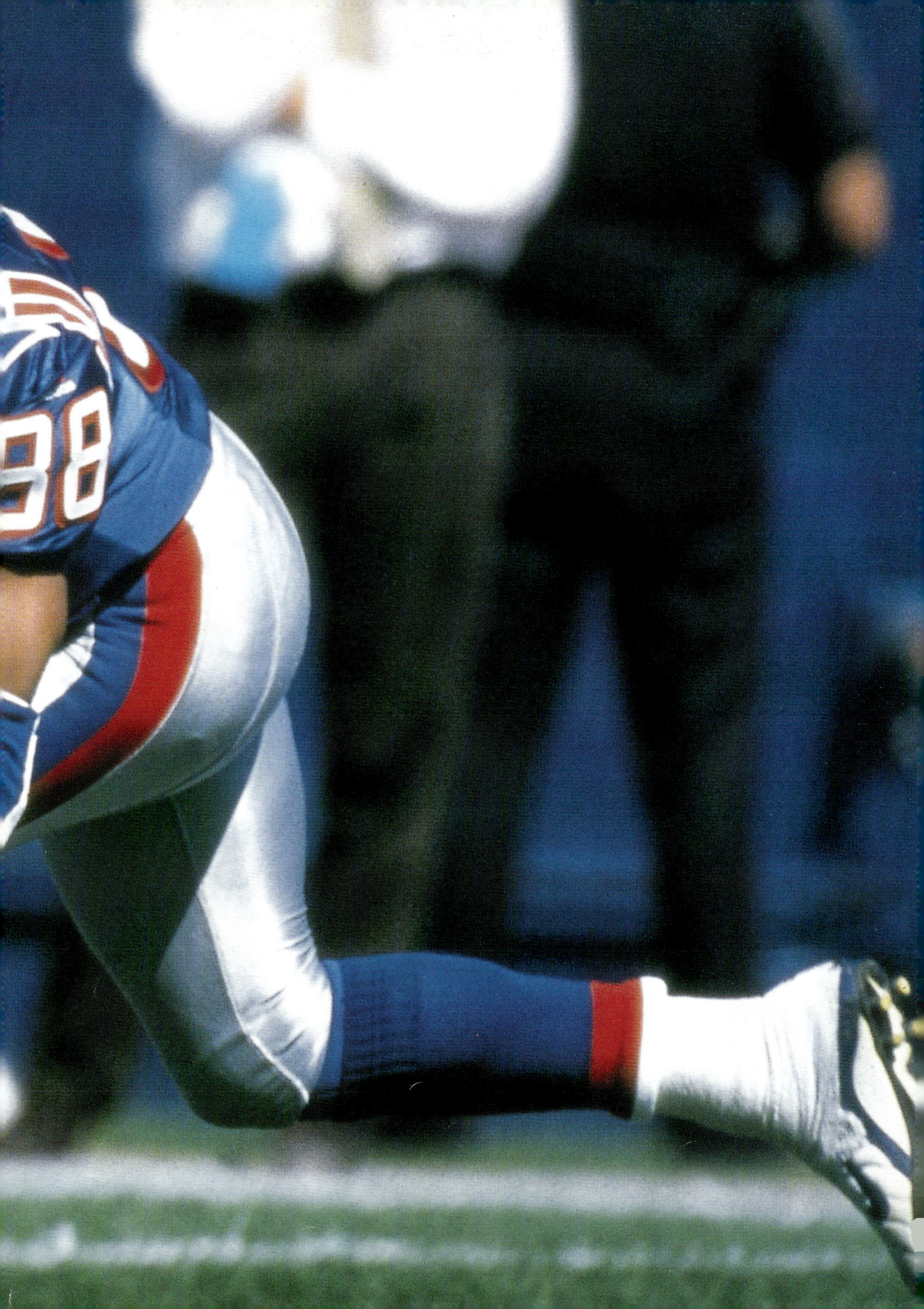

1998

Quarterback Drew Bledsoe shredded defenses with 3,633 passing yards.

combined for 24 points. From there, however, the Packers pulled away to win 35–21. The Patriots' remarkable run was over, and so was Bill Parcells's tenure with the Patriots.

Parcells wanted more control in personnel decisions, and he could get that with the Jets, who offered more money and team control to lure him to New York. Parcells accepted the offer, but since he was under contract in New England for another season, the Patriots received several future draft picks as compensation. With that, the Parcells era in New England came to an end.

BLEDSOE LEADS THE CHARGE

The Patriots next hired Pete Carroll, former defensive co-ordinator for the San Francisco 49ers. Although many fans lamented the loss of Parcells, the players looked upon the transition positively. "[Parcells's] gone, and we've moved on," Bledsoe said. "We're in the Pete Carroll era, and we're moving onward and upward."

With Carroll at the helm, New England earned a second straight AFC East title in 1997, finishing 10–6 after a 4–0 start. New England fans showed their appreciation for the Patriots' success in 1997 by turning out in record numbers over the course of the season.

Among the highlights fans were treated to was the play of defensive tackle Henry Thomas, who notched seven sacks—the most by a Patriots tackle in 17 years. The offense was also often spectacular, outscoring its opponents 130–40 in September, even with stars Glenn and Martin sidelined with injuries for much of the season.

New England's first playoff opponent was Miami, a familiar foe. The meeting would be the teams' third for the season and their second in a week. For the third time that year, New England triumphed, this time 17–3 in Miami. The following week, defenses dominated as the Steelers snuffed out the Patriots' Super Bowl hopes, 7–6.

After the season, Curtis Martin followed Parcells to New York as a free agent. Rookie halfback Robert Edwards filled in admirably in 1998, running for 1,115 yards and nine touchdowns. The big story in New England that year, however, was quarterback Drew Bledsoe, who orchestrated dramatic wins for the Patriots in critical back-to-back games late in the season.

Bledsoe's first miracle came against Miami. Trailing by four points late in the fourth quarter, Bledsoe threw a pass and struck his hand against a defender's helmet, breaking his right index finger. Using timeouts to rest his hand, Bledsoe led the Patriots 80 yards in less than three minutes, finishing the drive with a game-winning 25-yard touchdown strike to receiver Shawn Jefferson with just seconds left.

A week later, Bledsoe was at it again, this time leading his team to a 25–21 win over Buffalo with another touchdown pass on the final play of the game. "He's stepped up his game to be one of the game's big-time quarterbacks," said Rams linebacker Mike Jones. "He's become patient in the pocket, and he's got a rocket [arm]—he gets the ball anywhere on the field whenever he wants."

However, by the end of the season, Bledsoe was sidelined by the broken finger. Without their quarterback, the Patriots fell 25–10 to Jacksonville in the playoffs. Unfortunately, New

1999

Halfback Terry Allen led the team's rushing attack with 896 yards.

Drew Bledsoe led the Patriots with his poise under pressure.

One of the NFL's premier defensive backs, Lawyer Milloy.

Head coach Bill Belichick hoped to mold the Patriots into Super Bowl contenders.

England continued to suffer injuries even in the off-season. Rookie sensation Robert Edwards, fresh off his 1,000-yard season, dislocated his knee in a flag football game during Pro Bowl events in Hawaii. Edwards would miss an entire season as he worked to rehabilitate the knee.

Even without Edwards, though, the Patriots boasted a 6–2 record halfway through the 1999 season. Unfortunately, the promising start disappeared as the team fell into a puzzling late-season slide. After New England dropped to an 8–8 record and missed the playoffs, coach Pete Carroll was fired. "I'm proud of being 27–21 and making the playoffs the first two years I was here," said Carroll, "[but] I'll forever be disappointed we didn't win more."

The Patriots faithful looked for new coach Bill Belichick to lead proud New England to glory in the new century. With the Patriots scheduled to move into a new stadium in Foxboro in the year 2001, the team's future is a bright one. In fact, the day may soon come when these Patriots charge all the way to the NFL championship.